The Girl's Guide to

WEREWOLVES

Everything Charming about
These Shape-Shifters

by Jen Jones

CAPSTONE PRESS
a capstone imprint

Snap Books are published by Capstone Press,
151 Good Counsel Drive, P.O. Box 669, Mankato, Minnesota 56002.
www.capstonepub.com

Books published by Capstone Press are manufactured with paper
containing at least 10 percent post-consumer waste.

Library of Congress Cataloging-in-Publication Data
Jones, Jen.
  The Girl's guide to werewolves : everything charming about these shape-shifters / by Jen Jones.
    p. cm. — (Snap)
  Summary: "Describes the mystery, cool characteristics, and allure of werewolves, including historical and
contemporary examples"—Provided by publisher.
  Includes bibliographical references and index.
  ISBN 978-1-4296-5453-1 (library binding)
  1. Werewolves—Juvenile literature. I. Title. II. Series.

GR830.W4J66 2011
398.24'54—dc22   2010037842

Editorial Credits
Editor: Kathryn Clay
Designer: Tracy Davies
Media Researcher: Marcie Spence
Production Specialist: Laura Manthe

Photo Credits:
Alamy Images: Mary Evans Picture Library, 13, Redmond Durrell, 5; AP Images: 15;
Capstone Press: 9 (all), 17 (all); iStockphoto: Curt_Pickens, 25 (middle), logoff, 4, mrohner,
19 (top), Renphoto, 6, twildlife, 18, VikaValter, 19 (bottom); Kobal Collection, The: Wolfkill,
28 (bottom); Newscom: a11/Zuma Press, 29 (middle), Famous-Ace Pictures, 28 (top), Summit
Entertainment/Temple Hill Ent./Maverick Films/Imprint/French, Kimberly, 7, 21 (bottom),
Universal Pictures, 26, World History Archive, 27 (bottom); Shutterstock: Alhovik, cover
(scratches), Allyson Kitts, cover (house), balaikin, 19 (middle), Galushko Sergey, 27 (top),
JB Manning, 27 (middle), Kane513, 25 (bottom), Kynata, cover (girl silhouette), Myotis, 21
(top), Photosani, cover (wolf), 25 (top), S.M., 11; Supplied by Capital Pictures, 29 (bottom);
Wikimedia: 29 (top).

Printed in the United States of America in North Mankato, Minnesota.
092010
005933CGS11

Contents

Chapter 1
Full Moon Fever 4

Chapter 2
Howlin' History 10

Chapter 3
Beauty of the Beast 18

Quiz
Is Your BFF a She-Wolf? 22

Chapter 4
Who's Afraid of the Big Bad Wolf 24

Glossary.................................. 30

Read More 31

Internet Sites 31

Index....................................... 32

Chapter One

Full Moon Fever

Imagine being able to turn into a bird, snake, or other animal any time you want. Welcome to the world of **shape-shifters**. Perhaps the most famous form of shape-shifter is a powerful beast that is half man and half wolf. These creatures howl, hunt, and travel in packs.

Werewolves run wild at night.

During the day, werewolves look just like everyone else. Yet by night, they become hairy, hungry creatures on the hunt.

Werewolves can be born or made. They can transform at will or during a full moon. Some people become werewolves after being bitten or scratched by another werewolf. Other people are born werewolves. Still others are cursed. In the Demonata book series, the Grady family has a curse in their bloodline. Grady children turn into werewolves in their teen years.

How can you tell if you're facing a werewolf? Waiting for the moon to come out isn't going to help. While some people turn into werewolves during a full moon, others transform while under stress. Some can transform whenever they want!

Is that a wolf or a werewolf you hear?

FACT

One of the oldest known ways to become a werewolf is to drink water from the paw print left by a wolf.

shape-shifter: one that can change form or identity at will

How does one become a werewolf? Legends have varied over time. Years ago, people believed it was as easy as putting on a belt made of wolf skin. Still others say it can happen if a person is bitten or scratched by a werewolf.

For years, werewolves were often shown as scary and evil.

Sharp teeth are only one fearsome werewolf feature.

Yet recent books and movies have changed the way we look at them. Clever characters like Jacob Black in the Twilight series and Remus Lupin in the Harry Potter series have made werewolves into celebrities. Now they're heartthrobs and heroes! Whatever their nature, there is no doubt that werewolves are among the smartest, fiercest beasts in the bunch.

Thanks to their impressive makeover process, werewolves have been featured in movies, books, fairy tales, and TV shows. Turn the page to see werewolves who have become stars.

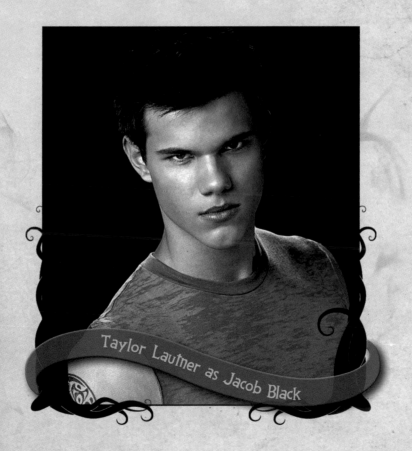

Taylor Lautner as Jacob Black

FOLLOW the FANTASY
Page-Turning Reads

Much of our understanding of werewolves comes from stories on the printed page. Werewolves are sometimes hairy and scary but never boring. It makes sense that these creatures are often featured in a good story. If you love things that howl and growl in the night, don't miss these page-turners.

Blood and Chocolate by Annette Curtis Klause

Can a werewolf have a normal life? Sixteen-year-old Vivian hopes so. After the death of her father, the pack leader, Vivian's life is filled with problems. A rival gang threatens to expose the pack's secret. An **alpha** werewolf wants to make Vivian his mate. And Vivian falls in love with a human. Will Vivian choose her pack or expose her secret for love?

alpha: a high-ranking member of a group

The Witchy Worries of Abbie Adams by Rhonda Hayter

It's not always easy being 11 years old, especially if you're Abbie Adams. Sure she's dealing with regular stuff like homework, mean teachers, and practicing for the school play. But most people don't know that she's a witch, and her younger brother is a werewolf. From time travel to hairy brothers, there's never a dull moment in this book!

Red Rider's Hood by Neal Shusterman

The classic fairy tale is all grown up in this twist on *Little Red Riding Hood*. Meet Red Rider. He's a boy with a hot red Mustang and a werewolf-hunting grandma. Lurking within Grandma's neighborhood is a dangerous gang known as the Wolves. To learn the Wolves' secrets, Red Rider goes undercover and joins the pack. Things get complicated when he learns they are werewolves.

Chapter Two

Howlin' History

Maybe you think that werewolves are purely make-believe. But plenty of people suspect that werewolves are all too real. In 1988 nearly 350,000 people called a hotline set up to promote the television show *Werewolf*. Many of the callers reported werewolf sightings.

Some people even claim to be werewolves!

Of course, werewolf sightings are nothing new. For hundreds of years, people all over the world have passed down real-life **lupine** legends. So are werewolves true creatures of the night, or do they simply make a good story?

Do werewolves go "bump" in the night?

lupine: having wolflike qualities

THE FIRST WEREWOLF

Werewolf legends began in early Greek **mythology**. It all started with the Greek king Lycaon. To punish Lycaon for his cruel ways, the gods turned him into a wolf. Stories differ on how Lycaon was transformed, but one thing is certain—he is considered the first werewolf. Lycaon's name inspired the word "lycanthropy," which means a magical ability to become a wolf. Ovid's famous poem "Metamorphoses" also tells his story.

Many Europeans believed that werewolves were taken over by the devil.

Many werewolf stories also came from common beliefs during the Middle Ages. Throughout Europe, serial killings and actual wolf attacks led to the spread of werewolf fears.

Werewolf legends have been around for centuries.

In 1589 German farmer Peter Stumpp was put on trial for being a werewolf. Stumpp admitted to killing 16 people, but he said it was the devil's doing. He claimed the devil had given him a belt. The belt turned him into a greedy, devouring wolf with a huge body, sharp teeth, and strong paws.

mythology: a collection of myths

REAL-LIFE WEREWOLVES

Werewolf fever continued into modern day. In the 1970s, Canadian doctors reported several cases of wolflike behavior. The patients shared stories of howling at the moon, discovering strange powers, and sleeping in graveyards.

In 2007 Danny Ramos Gomez was featured on a TV show. He had earned the nickname "Wolf Man," due to a medical problem. A disease nicknamed the "werewolf syndrome" left his body covered with hair. Though a rare condition, people throughout the world have reported carrying the disease.

The werewolf craze appears to be invading high schools as well.

Recent news reports have shared claims of real-life teen werewolves. In San Antonio, Texas, at least six wolf packs are said to be on the loose. The packs claim to have up to 20 werewolves each. So are they true werewolves or just teens copying their favorite flicks? No one knows for sure. But the growing number of werewolf reports definitely blurs the line between fact and fantasy.

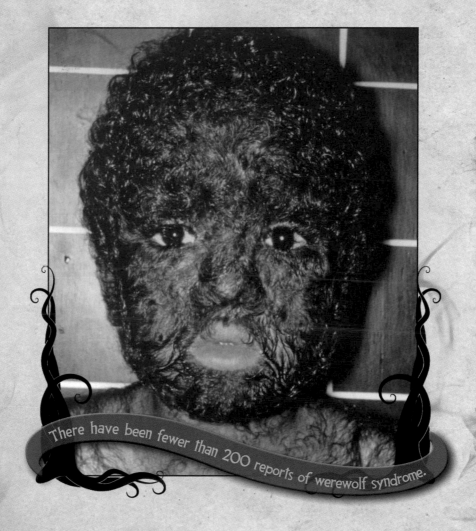

There have been fewer than 200 reports of werewolf syndrome.

FOLLOW the FANTASY On Screen

For years Hollywood has been putting werewolves in the spotlight. Some of the first werewolf flicks were *The Werewolf* (1913), *Werewolf of London* (1935), and *The Wolf Man* (1941). *I Was a Teen Werewolf* (1957) and *Teen Wolf* (1985) still hold their appeal as werewolf movies today. Though the special effects have gotten better over time, the excitement and mystery remains the same. See their appeal for yourself in these modern werewolf flicks:

The Twilight Saga

Forget Edward Cullen. For werewolf fans, "Team Jacob" is the place to be. The movies are based on the popular book series by Stephenie Meyer. Audiences are introduced to human Bella, vampire Edward, and werewolf Jacob. The trio becomes part of a battle between vampires and werewolves in their small Washington town.

 ## Werewolf of Fever Swamp

Twilight isn't the only book featuring werewolves to be turned into a movie. Enter *Werewolf of Fever Swamp*, based on R. L. Stine's Goosebumps series. The movie tells the story of Grady, a young boy whose family moves to the swamps of Florida. His new town is full of werewolf mysteries and legends, not to mention a Swamp Hermit.

 ## The Brothers Grimm

This action-packed film follows Wilhelm and Jacob Grimm, played by Matt Damon and Heath Ledger. The brothers get mixed up in a tale of black magic. They face an immortal witch, a werewolf, and other supernatural creatures. The brothers must learn to recognize what is real and what is fantasy in order to break the witch's spell.

Chapter Three

Beauty of the Beast

Much like their on-screen images, werewolves really are larger than life. In fact, legends tell us that they can be up to 8 feet (2.4 meters) tall and have strength to match their size. So what else sets werewolves apart? There are plenty of ways to spot a werewolf, even if you're not running with the pack. Find useful clues in the following ferocious features.

Can you tell the difference between wolves and werewolves?

Glowing Eyes: Keep a look out for glowing eyes in the night. Some werewolves have humanlike brown or green eyes. Others have bright gold eyes, like Michael Jackson's character in the music video for "Thriller." When in human form, a werewolf might also have eyebrows that meet in the middle.

Fur Coat: Werewolves are covered in fur that comes out in full force when they shape-shift. Even as humans, the fur is always there. It just hides under the skin's surface. Many werewolves also sprout whiskers when they transform.

Sharp Teeth: Werewolves usually grow sharp fanglike teeth. All the better to tear into their prey, my dear!

Pointy Ears: Like most canines, werewolves can hear high-pitched and faraway sounds better than most. Perhaps that's why their ears turn pointy when they shape-shift. They're zoning in on their target!

Big Claws: Werewolves grow large, C-shaped paws designed for capturing victims. Long, oval-shaped fingernails also help them dig into their catch.

WAKE UP, WOLF

In many cases, people discover their werewolf side during a full moon.

When this werewolf change happens for the first time, it's known as an awakening. Often, this can happen during the teen years. In the Twilight series, every member of the Quileute wolf pack transforms as a teen. Pack leader Sam Uley is the first and the oldest at age 19. Fifteen-year-old Seth Clearwater is the youngest.

FACT

The Twilight wolves can transform, or "phase", whenever they want.

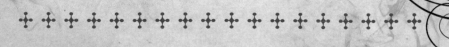

Are you afraid of a full moon?

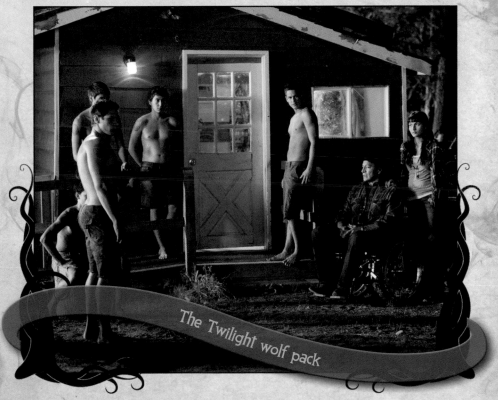

The Twilight wolf pack

QUIZ: Is Your BFF a She-Wolf?

Do you think your BFF could be a werewolf in disguise? Take this quiz and find out—if you dare!

When your BFF wants to relax, she:

a) goes for a run through the woods.

b) gets a manicure. Her nails are always so long!

c) lounges by the pool.

d) takes a long afternoon nap in a dark corner.

Your BFF can't stop talking about:

a) Taylor Lautner

b) Tyler Posey

c) Nick Jonas

d) Robert Pattinson

Your BFF decides to get a dog. She adopts a:

a) German Shepherd

b) huskie

c) fluffy Pomeranian

d) bloodhound

Who's your BFF's favorite Twilight character?

a) Jacob Black
b) Leah Clearwater
c) Bella Swan
d) Edward Cullen

Where would your BFF love to get a part-time job?

a) a dog pound
b) a veterinarian's office
c) a bookstore
d) a blood bank

What is your BFF's favorite werewolf book?

a) Not sure—she always changes the subject when I bring it up.
b) She loves any story with a werewolf in it.
c) She'll read a werewolf book but doesn't have any favorites.
d) Books about werewolves? She hates them!

Look through your answers to see if your BFF is leader of the wolf pack. If you circled:

Mostly As: Your BFF definitely plays for Team Jacob.

Mostly Bs: You may want to avoid moonlight strolls with your BFF. It's possible she's a werewolf.

Mostly Cs: No need to worry. Your BFF is human as can be.

Mostly Ds: She's not a werewolf, but you'll want to keep some garlic nearby. It sounds like she might be a vampire!

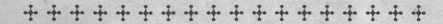

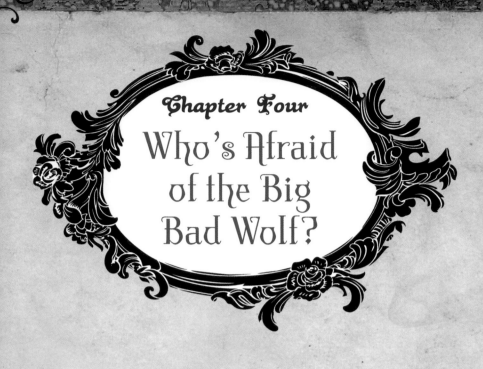

Chapter Four

Who's Afraid of the Big Bad Wolf?

Killing animals, and sometimes people, is all part of werewolves' animal **instincts**. But because they are part human, werewolves are expected to follow human laws. As such, they often get the criminal treatment. In France during the 1500s, thousands of suspected werewolves were put on trial for attacking villagers.

Yet werewolves can also use their amazing powers for protecting others. Anyone who's read the Twilight books knows that they have a soft side. Whether used for good or evil, there is no doubt that werewolves have some serious strengths.

instinct: behavior that is natural rather than learned

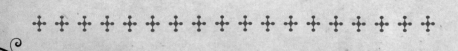

Shape Shifting: Perhaps the coolest thing that werewolves do is shape-shift from human form into wolf form. For many werewolves, it happens automatically during a full moon. Others can do it on command. The idea of shape-shifting started with American Indians. Many of their legends describe humans turning into animals. These people are called skin-walkers.

The Need for Speed: Werewolves run with unbelievable speed on all fours like wolves. In the Twilight series, Jacob and his fellow werewolves race through the forest in search of vampires. Though vampires are also known for their speed, there is usually no outrunning a werewolf.

Strong Senses: Imagine being able to see, smell, or hear like a superhero. Werewolves can do just that. From seeing in the dark to hearing things from far away, werewolves' senses are super sharp.

Werewolf Weaknesses

Catching a werewolf is no easy task. But killing one is even harder. What is powerful enough to take down a werewolf? Like zombies, the most successful way to kill a werewolf is to cut off its head! Yet there are other ways to stop a werewolf in its tracks. Keep reading to find out what makes werewolves weak.

Would you know how to fend off a werewolf?

Full Moon: For shape-shifters, a full moon can certainly be an unwelcome sight. Imagine if you were hanging out with friends or had an important event and forgot what day it was. Full moons are known for causing strange happenings, and werewolf transformations are no exception. The first movie to show a werewolf changing under a full moon was 1941's *The Wolf Man*.

Silver: Regular weapons won't harm a werewolf. Silver bullets and knives are the only weapons that can kill or cause injury to a werewolf. For many werewolves, their skin will burn if they even touch silver. In the comedy flick *My Mom's a Werewolf*, Harry is a werewolf who refuses to use silverware when eating. He meets his end when stabbed by a silver knife.

Monkshood: An ingredient often used in witches' brew, monkshood is said to have first come from the drool of Hercules' evil three-headed dog. Some say anyone who eats monkshood will turn into a werewolf. The more common belief is that monkshood is actually poisonous werewolves. The jury is still out on this toxic plant's powers.

Sticky Scars: When werewolves get hurt, their scars can often be seen even when they are in human form. Telltale scars make them easier to spot.

WEREWOLVES' YEARBOOK

Biggest Heartthrob
Jacob Black (Twilight series)

This werewolf doesn't win Bella's heart, but he's definitely not hurting for fans. They're all Team Jacob!

Most Valuable Player
Scott Howard (Teen Wolf)

Follow Scott's transformation from scrawny benchwarmer to king of slam dunks.

Most Likely Hero
Link (*The Legend of Zelda: Twilight Princess*)

This part wolf/part human is all hero. You control Link as he saves his homeland from the evil Twilight Realm in this wolf-packed video game.

Perfect Theme Song
She-Wolf by Shakira

This chart-topping hit tells the story of living life as a human in disguise.

Best Wizarding Werewolf
Remus Lupin (The Harry Potter series)

Though a werewolf, Remus was able to teach Harry Potter the powerful Patronus spell.

GLOSSARY

alpha (AL-fuh)—a high-ranking member of a group of animals

canine (KAY-nine)—a dog or doglike animal

immortal (i-MOR-tuhl)—able to live forever

instinct (IN-stingkt)—behavior that is natural rather than learned

lupine (LOO-pine)—having wolflike qualities

mythology (mi-THOL-uh-jee)—a collection of myths

shape~shifter (SHAYP-SHIFT-ur)—one that can change form or identity at will

syndrome (SIHN-drohm)—a group of at least three signs that occur together and characterize a disease

READ MORE

Ganeri, Anita and illustrated by David West.
Werewolves and Other Shapeshifters. The Dark Side.
New York: PowerKids Press, 2011.

Troupe, Thomas Kingsley and illustrated by D.C. Ice.
Legend of the Werewolf. Legend Has It. Mankato, Minn.:
Picture Window Books, 2011.

Weber, Belinda. *Fabulous and Monstrous Beasts.* New York:
Kingfisher, 2008.

INTERNET SITES

FactHound offers a safe, fun way to find Internet sites
related to this book. All of the sites on FactHound have
been researched by our staff.

Here's all you do:

Visit *www.facthound.com*

Type in this code: 9781429654531

Super-cool stuff! Check out projects, games and lots more at
www.capstonekids.com

INDEX

Black, Jacob, 7, 23, 25, 28

Demonata (series), 5

full moons, 5, 20, 25, 27

Gomez, Danny Ramos, 14

Harry Potter (series), 7, 29

Lupin, Remus, 7, 29

quiz, 22–23

Stumpp, Peter, 13

Twilight
 books, 7, 20, 24, 28
 movies, 16, 25

Werewolf (TV show), 10
werewolf syndrome, 14, 15

werewolves
 becoming a, 5, 6
 books about, 5, 7, 8–9,
  28, 29
 characteristics, 13, 18,
  19, 24–25
 hunting, 4, 5
 legends, 6, 11, 12,
  17, 18
 movies about, 16–17,
  25, 27, 28, 29
 music about, 19, 29
 packs, 4, 8, 9, 15, 18,
  20, 23
 sightings of, 10–11
 transforming, 5, 12, 13,
  19, 20, 25, 27, 28
 trials, 13, 24
 video games about, 29
 weaknesses, 26–27